Flying into the 21st Century

by Gail K. Gordon

Editorial Offices: Glenview, Illinois • Parsippany, New Jersey • New York, New York
Sales Offices: Needham, Massachusetts • Duluth, Georgia • Glenview, Illinois
Coppell, Texas • Ontario, California • Mesa, Arizona

ISBN: 0-328-13588-7

The First Airplane Passenger

The Wright brothers may have invented the airplane, but it was a friend of theirs who opened the era for airplane passengers. Charley Furnas, a mechanic by profession, was an airplane enthusiast who enjoyed assisting the Wrights in his spare time. In 1908, the brothers worked on building an airplane that could carry a pilot and one passenger to fulfill a U.S. Army request. At first, they used a sandbag in the new passenger seat to see how the weight of a passenger might affect the flight.

Finally, on May 14, 1908, the famous brothers were ready to carry their first real passenger. They decided to thank Furnas for all his help by giving him the honor. Furnas flew a distance of 800 feet with Wilbur Wright at the controls, and he then went on a two-mile flight with Orville. Although he didn't go very far and carried no baggage or ticket, Charley Furnas will always be the first American air passenger.

Preparing for the Flight

Air travel has changed a lot in the nearly one hundred years since Charley Furnas first flew. Come find out what air travel is like today by following our imaginary 21st-century traveling family, the Garcías, on an airplane voyage.

Grandma García, Mom, Dad, and their 12-year-old son Charlie live in Chicago, Illinois. Today they're catching an airline flight to Denver, Colorado. Of course, they could drive, but that would mean more than fifteen hours of travel time each way. They only have a few days to spend on this trip. Taking a commercial airliner from one airport to the other is the best way for the Garcías to get where they want to go in the time they have.

While they are traveling together, each member of the García family has a different reason for going to Denver. Grandma will visit her sister. Mother is on a business trip, and Father wants to see his brother. Charlie wants to spend a day at a park he's read about. Like most people, the Garcías fly for business, to see family, and to enjoy leisure time.

Grandma remembers the days before personal computers and buying tickets over the phone with a credit card. She tells Charlie that you used to go to the office of a travel **agent** to buy airline tickets. For this trip, she bought the airline tickets for the family on the airline's Web site using her computer. Unlike years ago, the Garcías don't have paper tickets they might lose or forget at home. The airline issued them electronic tickets, or e-tickets, instead. The online reservation was registered, and when the family arrives at the airport, they will print out their own boarding passes. Before they left home, the Garcías used their home computer to check the weather in Denver and monitor their flight status. The airline's Web site told them that their flight is scheduled to leave on time.

Travelers rarely go to a travel agent just to buy airline tickets anymore.

A neighbor drove the family from their home to an airport in Chicago. They arrive at the airline's passenger and baggage check-in counter more than an hour before their flight. Since the Garcías have e-tickets, they can use a self-service **kiosk** to check themselves in and print out boarding passes.

Grandma first slides in the credit card she bought the tickets with as identification. The García's flight information appears on the screen. Grandma checks that it's correct and enters in that they have two bags to check. An airline agent takes the family's two suitcases. He attaches tags that are marked "DEN," the symbol for Denver's airport, and puts the luggage on a conveyor belt that will take the bags to a screening area. There the luggage will be X-rayed and perhaps searched by hand. The luggage screeners make sure that there are no explosives or other harmful materials in baggage.

Would you rather serve yourself at the kiosk, or wait in line for an agent?

Then the Garcías proceed to the security checkpoint. There, each person presents a picture ID with a boarding pass to a security agent. All the family's carry-on items—laptop computers, purses, backpacks full of snacks and magazines, and even coats and jackets—must be checked before the family can go to the boarding gate. A conveyer belt moves these carry-on items through an X-ray machine that allows security personnel to see inside everything. If a pocketknife, pair of scissors, or anything else is found that's disallowed on an airplane, the security workers **confiscate** it.

The Garcías then each take turns walking through a metal detector. This prevents someone from boarding the plane with a gun, knife, or other weapon on their person. When Dad goes through, the metal detector beeps loudly! An agent asks him to empty his pockets into a bin. After fishing out his keys and placing them in the container, Dad successfully passes through the metal detector on his second try.

Security checks take time, but they make air travel safer.

After going through security, the Garcías check one of the monitors that lists the departure times of flights and their gate numbers. If a flight is delayed or canceled, that information will appear on the monitor. Gate changes appear on the monitors as well. The Garcías' flight is still on time.

By the time the Garcías walk to the gate, an airline agent is already giving instructions on how to board the plane. Grandma remembers having to walk outside to board a plane. The passengers walked across the **tarmac**—no matter the weather— and up a flight of portable stairs that had been rolled into place to allow access to the door. Today the Garcías simply walk through a jetway, an enclosed tunnel, to board the airplane. Once inside, they find their seats, stow their carry-on items, and settle in for the flight.

Take-Off!

The Garcías are traveling in a mid-sized commercial jet. Charlie can see part of the jet engine outside his window. Grandma can remember taking flights on planes that had propellers instead of jet engines. In fact, many smaller planes that fly short routes still have propellers. The ride is much noisier on those planes!

As the jet **taxis** down the runway, a flight attendant directs the passengers' attention to the several small television monitors that slowly drop down from the ceiling. A video explaining the operation of the seatbelts, the exits, and the emergency breathing equipment begins. Grandma reminds Charlie that it wasn't long ago that the flight attendants themselves would instruct the passengers. On some planes, they still do. When the video is complete, Charlie pulls a folder from his seat pocket. It shows diagrams that explain how the emergency exits and other safety equipment work.

As the jet gains speed for take-off, Charlie feels pushed back into his seat. This feeling increases as the jet leaves the ground and climbs at a steep angle into the sky. Once the plane stops its steep ascent, Charlie feels pretty normal. He does feel some pressure in his ears, like when swimming underwater. A big yawn gets rid of it. Soon, the pilot comes on the intercom and tells the passengers that the plane has reached its **cruising altitude.** He adds that the flight will last two hours and should reach Denver on time.

Cruising

The pilot is speaking from the commercial jet's cockpit. The pilot and co-pilot are surrounded by brightly lit panels that display essential data. The crew in the cockpit can see up-to-the-second information on the aircraft's altitude and speed, how much fuel it's using, its orientation in relation to the horizon, cabin air pressure, exterior temperature and wind speed, and more. In fact, much of the navigation of today's commercial jets is automated. Based on flying conditions, the plane is programmed with the best route to get it from its point of departure to its arrival point. Of course, the crew is trained to take over manual control of the plane if that's necessary.

The route the Garcías are flying today is an often-traveled one. These set air routes are called airways, and they have a designated miles-wide width and a particular altitude. This means that jets flying along airways can cross each other just as elevated highways cross lower-lying roadways. Charlie looks out of the small window at the blue sky above the layer of clouds. He looks for other planes, but doesn't see any.

Soon the flight attendants are in the aisles, serving beverages and snack packets to the passengers. The Garcías and the other passengers sip their drinks, nibble their snacks, and settle in for what looks to be a smooth flight. The pilot has announced that no **turbulence** is anticipated during the flight. Mother pulls down the tray table in front of her, sets up her laptop computer, and works on a report. Father tilts back his seat, puts on earphones plugged into the seat's armrest, and closes his eyes as he listens to music. Grandma makes a quick phone call to her sister, using the phone on the seat back in front of her. Charlie starts to flip through the magazine he brought. Then the small television monitors drop out of the ceiling again. Charlie looks for the earphones in his seat pocket as Grandma tells him that when she was a young woman, they didn't have movies, music, and telephones on airplanes.

After watching the inflight programming, Charlie notices that the plane is slowly descending. He looks out the window as the plane breaks through a cloud layer. Charlie can see the ground far below. At first, he can't make out many details, but eventually he sees farms, towns, and highways. As the plane nears Denver's airport, Charlie can count the number of swimming pools in a suburban neighborhood.

Landing

As they circle above the airport, the captain comes back on the intercom. He tells the passengers that they'll be landing in a few minutes, at 2:35 P.M., local time. Charlie looks at his watch. It says 3:30. Grandma notices Charlie's confused look. She reminds him that Denver is in the Mountain time zone. It is an hour earlier than Chicago's Central time zone. They both smile as they reset their watches.

The flight attendants walk up and down the aisle, preparing the passengers for landing. Passengers are reminded to buckle their seatbelts, turn off their computers and other electronic devices, and put their tray tables and seatbacks up. It's time to land the airliner.

In the cockpit, the crew is also preparing to land. They're communicating with the air traffic

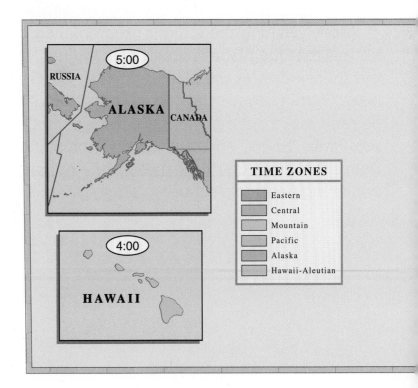

controllers in the tower at the airport. Air traffic control plays a crucial role in air travel. The people in the control tower at the airport monitor all the flights departing, arriving, and flying in the airspace around the airport. It's an air traffic controller's job to keep aircraft at a safe distance from one another.

As the Garcías' flight begins its approach to the airport, the pilot must follow the directions of the control tower regarding speed, position, and altitude. The controllers will direct the pilot to a clear runway. The air traffic controllers don't depend solely on the electronic tracking system. They also use binoculars to scan the sky and the runways. Once the controllers decide it's safe, they grant the pilot final clearance to land. The Garcías' airplane safely sets down on the runway, with only a few bumps!

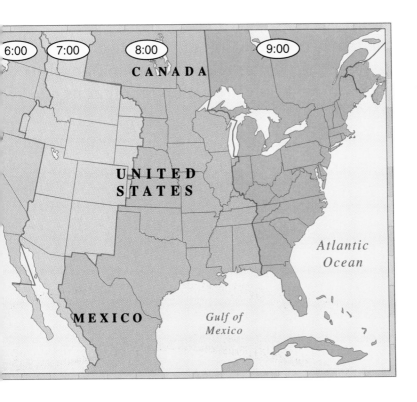

After a short taxi, the aircraft comes to a stop. A two-bell signal from the captain alerts everyone that the plane is safely parked at the gate and that they are free to unbuckle their seatbelts and gather their belongings. Father pops open the bin above his seat and grabs his jacket. Mother, Grandma, and Charlie pull their carry-on bags out from under the seats in front of them. They file off the plane and into Denver's airport, where signs direct them to baggage claim. At the carousel in the baggage claim area, they'll pick up their checked luggage. It's been a smooth flight!

Behind the Scenes

You have read about the airline agents, security workers, pilots, flight attendants, and air traffic controllers who worked to make the Garcías' flight run smoothly. These are not the only people who helped the family get from Chicago to Denver, however. When the Garcías' flight landed in Denver, a whole crew of workers were waiting for it at its assigned gate.

Baggage handlers were there to open the cargo hold and begin unloading luggage, even before all the passengers had departed from the plane. The baggage handlers sort each piece of checked luggage according to the aiport code on the bag's luggage tag. The tags on the Garcías' bags say DEN, which means "Denver." Their luggage was put on a cart and taken to baggage claim inside the Denver airport. Other passengers may have been catching flights to different cities, so their bags were sent to the proper airplane and loaded into its cargo hold.

The plane on which the Garcías traveled to Denver will probably not stay in Denver. In a short time, the plane will be serviced and ready to carry passengers to some other destination. A crew of mechanics, cleaners, and other service personnel work quickly to ready the aircraft for its next flight. Mechanics check to make sure the airplane is safe to fly. Workers fill the plane's fuel tanks. Cleaners go through the cabins, picking up any trash and collecting newspapers, magazines, and other items passengers may have left behind.

Soon the plane is ready for another take-off. Other families are ready to board and experience the adventure of modern air travel.

Air Travel in the Future

What will air travel be like for future passengers? Do you think you'll see as much change in air travel over your lifetime as Charlie's grandmother has?

Computers will likely play an even bigger role in future air travel. Engineers will depend on computers to help them design better aircraft. Scientists are also always looking for new materials that will make an aircraft lighter and stronger. Even today, lightweight materials that will withstand significant heat are being tested for use in extremely fast-traveling aircraft.

Perhaps the most exciting future possibility is that someday ordinary people might not only travel in aircraft, but in spacecraft. The first tourist in space was sixty-year-old Dennis Tito of California. He paid $20 million to fly to the International Space Station and back in a Russian rocket in 2001. He probably felt the same kind of excitement that Charlie Furnas felt in 1908.

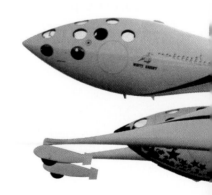

SpaceShipOne

In 2004 Mike Melville brought passenger space travel one step closer to reality. As pilot of the revolutionary SpaceShipOne, Melville became the first civilian astronaut to take a private vehicle into space. On Melville's first flight in SpaceShipOne he left Earth's atmosphere and reached an altitude of sixty-two miles.

A private company is already working to build a fleet of SpaceShipOne-type spacecraft. The company sees a future when ordinary people—like the Garcías—will be able to travel into space to pursue science, business, or pleasure.

Like SpaceShipOne, proposed passenger spaceships will be carried aloft by a carrier plane that takes off from a regular runway. When the flight reaches an altitude of about ten miles, the real countdown to space will begin. The craft will separate from the carrier and soar upward into black star-filled space. The first flights will last only a few minutes, but passengers will experience weightlessness and be able to look back at distant Earth.

SpaceShipOne sits atop its carrier plane White Knight.

The Garcías had to set their watches back an hour when arriving in Denver because they crossed into another time zone as they flew from Chicago. Now let's send Charlie on a longer trip and see what time it is along the way.

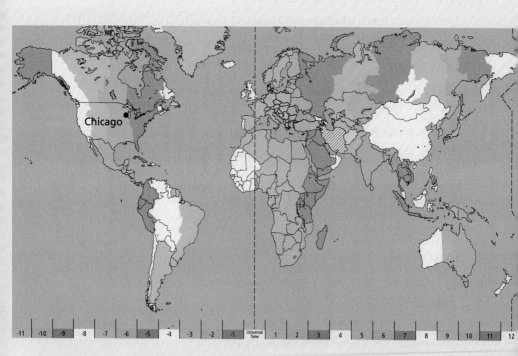

-11 | -10 | -9 | -8 | -7 | -6 | -5 | -4 | -3 | -2 | -1 | Universal Time | 1 | 2 | 3 | 4 | 5 | 6 | 7 | 8 | 9 | 10 | 11 | 12

1. First, use the map on these pages to choose six destinations for Charlie to visit. Make sure each place is in a different time zone.

2. Every day, no matter where he's traveling, Charlie calls home to his family in Chicago, Illinois. They expect his call every evening at 8 P.M. their time. Check the map for Chicago's time zone.

3. Now help Charlie call home while he's in each of the places you chose in step 1. What time in his location does he need to call home so that it's 8 P.M. in Chicago? Determine Charlie's local call time for each of his six destinations. Happy traveling!

Glossary

agent *n.* a person who does business for someone else; a representative.

altitude *n.* height above Earth's surface.

confiscate *v.* to take away by authority.

cruising *adj.* moving at the normal speed for traveling.

kiosk *n.* small structure with open sides, usually a place to post information.

tarmac *n.* paved surface, such as a road or runway.

taxis *v.* moves an aircraft slowly on the ground.

turbulence *n.* rough air encountered in flight, often caused by storms or other windy conditions.